St Stephen's Handbook for Altar Servers

D0547554

St Stephen, Deacon and Martyr, Patron of Altar Servers

St Stephen's Handbook for Altar Servers

Edward Matthews

with the Archconfraternity of St Stephen

First Published by Wm Collins 1986, London
This edition first published in 1994
Reprinted 1995

Gracewing
Fowler Wright Books
Southern Avenue, Leominster
Herefordshire HR6 0QF

Gracewing Books are distributed

In New Zealand by
Catholic Supplies Ltd
80 Adelaide Rd
Wellington
New Zealand

In Australia by
Charles Paine Pty
8 Ferris Street
North Parramatta
NSW 2151 Australia

In Canada by
Meakin & Assoc.
Unit 17, 81, Auriga Drive
Nepean
Ontario KZE 7YS
Canada

In U.S.A. by
Morehouse Publishing
P.O. Box 1321
Harrisburg
PA 17105
U.S.A.

Nihil obstat Father Anton Cowan, Censor
Imprimatur Basil Hume OSB
 Archbishop of Westminster
Westminster 12 June 1986

The Nihil obstat and Imprimatur are a declaration that a book or pamphlet is considered to be free from doctrinal or moral error. It is not implied that those who have granted the Nihil obstat and Imprimatur agree with the contents, opinions or statements expressed.

Cover photograph by Carlos Reyes
Interior illustrations by Jayne Morris & John Wallace

Printed and bound by The Cromwell Press

ISBN 0 85244 277 7

Contents

Preface

Altar servers play a most important part in the Church's liturgy. Good servers enable us all, bishops, priests and laity to celebrate the Mass and the other sacraments with a spirit of prayer. This means that altar servers, too, should be prayerful people and be aware of the wonderful gifts God gives us in the liturgy. For well over eighty years the Archconfraternity of St Stephen has worked for the highest standards in serving the liturgy. I therefore welcome this entirely new edition of the Handbook, and I hope it will be not only a guide to the correct way of serving, but also a key to a deeper understanding of what we are really doing when we come together to worship God.

I thank the Archconfraternity for the invaluable work it has done and wish it every blessing for even greater success in the future.

✠ Basil Hume
Archbishop of Westminster

Chapter 1
Serving the Church

Sunday Morning

It's Sunday morning at the parish church. People are arriving for Mass. Men and women, boys and girls, young and old.

Some come as families, mothers and fathers with their children. Others are walking along to the church with their friends. Many come alone. Often the priest is at the door to welcome them all.

All of them will soon be gathered together as one family, the family of God. It is the Mass which makes this happen.

Inside the church there is a lot of activity before the Mass starts. People are buying the Catholic newspapers. Men and women (called ushers) are helping new arrivals find seats and they give them hymn books, or leaflets, so that everyone will be able to take part in the Mass.

The musicians are tuning up their instruments. A sacristan is putting out the bread and wine on a special table in preparation for the offertory procession. A reader is checking the Lectionary to make sure it is open at the correct page.

And altar servers are busy too. One is lighting the candles while another places the chalice on the side table.

There are other people we cannot see who have helped prepare for this Mass. For example, the man who polishes the floor of the church, and the lady who arranges the flowers, not to mention the one who washes the altar cloths.

Many different people use their talents to make the Mass a real family celebration — the celebration of God's family.

At Mass we help each other pray to the Father

Altar Servers

Everybody has a part to play. We are all called upon to answer the responses, join in the prayers, make gestures like the sign of the cross, kneeling, or sitting.

A few people have special tasks. Among these are the altar servers. You and me.

Server is a good word because it really tells us what the job is — to serve, to help, to assist.

In fact, everyone in the church is a server. We all serve each other. No matter who we are, we should help each other.

At Mass we help each other pray to the Father. We will say more about this later in the book.

The name 'altar server' means that most of our serving happens at, or near, the altar. We help the priest by holding the Missal for him, carrying the water and wine when they are needed, and many other actions like that.

Though the altar is the place around which we do most serving, there are times when we will leave the altar altogether. For example, at the beginning of Mass we may walk all round the church in procession. On Palm Sunday we may start the service in another building apart from the church.

Altar servers have a lot of interesting and exciting jobs to do. Most of these are ceremonies. They give the Mass greater solemnity and through them we are all helped to pray.

Jesus, the first of all servers

We have seen, in a very general way, what an altar server is and how the server is part of the whole community. Let's take a closer look.

Anyone who is a Christian has to be a server; we should all be at the service of each other. The reason is clear. When we were baptised we received a share in the life of Jesus Christ who was always serving other people. If we share his life then we should live like him, serving others.

Jesus came into this world to serve us. He himself said he 'came not to be served but to serve'. He came for us, to bring us forgiveness of our sins, to give us a new and never-ending life. He accomplished this when he died on the cross and rose from the dead.

Just before Jesus was arrested, while he was at the Last Supper with his friends, he did something which took them completely by surprise. But it was Jesus' way of showing them — and us — what he wants all Christians to do.

Before they started eating and drinking, Jesus picked up a jug of water and a large bowl and began washing the feet of his friends.

Washing feet like this was not so unusual. The roads of

We must serve each other as Jesus has served us

Israel were dusty and people wore sandals so their feet got dirty. Rich people often saw to it that the feet of their guests were washed when they arrived in the house. This was a sign of welcome. But the rich people did not do the washing themselves: they had servants to do it for them.

Imagine how Peter felt. Nobody as important as Jesus should kneel in front of him and wash *his* feet! That was a job for paid servants. So he tried to stop Jesus.

Jesus would not let him. He told Peter that this was something he must do, because he had come into the world to serve others. 'And what is more,' Jesus said, 'I have done this now as an example to you. You must copy me.'

This is an example for all followers of Christ. We must serve each other as Jesus has served us.

We all serve each other

Just before Communion, we give each other the Sign of Peace.

Jesus said, 'Love your neighbour as yourself.' Loving means wishing peace for our neighbour. It means wishing to do for our neighbour all that will make him or her truly happy. In other words, we Christians are at the service of one another.

Therefore, at Sunday Mass, many people are doing different jobs. We are serving each other.

The lady who reads the first Bible reading from the Lectionary is helping everyone to hear God's message. The man who conducts the singers is helping us all to sing to God and to praise him.

The priest serves, too. He serves everybody by leading us, helping us to worship and praise God as one people.

We, the altar servers, are helping the priest to do his part well. Not only the priest: our work, our serving, help everybody who is in the church to pray better and worship God together.

We all serve as a team

Each person has a job of service to do. Though each job is concerned with one part, or one aspect, of the Mass, each of those jobs links up with all the others.

It is a bit like a football team. Goalkeeper, striker, midfield, sweeper — all have their particular positions to play. If every player does their own part well, they unite with the others to produce a winning team.

St Paul the Apostle described the Church as a body with its different parts. Each part — arms, legs, eyes and so forth — has a particular job to do. When all the parts, or members, are working together properly the whole body works well.

St Paul gave the body a name — Christ. Because of our baptism we all share the life of Jesus Christ. Doing our own particular works of service (like altar serving) helps God's people really become — and act like — the body of Christ.

Altar serving is important

To be an altar server is important. We do things which build up the Church, the body of Christ. Working as a team with other ministers (the name we give to people like readers, priests, collectors), servers have special responsibilities which only we can carry out.

Altar serving is a gift

Building up the Body of Christ and making sure it works well is a job directed by the Holy Spirit. All people in the Church are given a gift, a talent, which they can use for the benefit of the Church.

Serving at the altar is one of those gifts.

The Holy Spirit has given us this gift. He is the one who calls us to this service in a way that is quite personal and special.

When we serve at the altar we are answering that call.

Altar serving is a privilege and an honour. Any gift of the Spirit must be so. Therefore we are happy and proud, in a quiet, humble sort of way, that the Holy Spirit should have chosen us for this particular service.

From this we can get an idea of what a good server should be like. Quiet, gentle, happy, ready to be of help, aware of our responsibility to everyone in the Church.

Serving never stops

The gifts the Holy Spirit gives us are not just for Mass and the other celebrations in Church. He wants us to put them to work in our daily lives as well. The work of Jesus Christ is going on all the time.

The Mass is a mirror of the Church. It reflects the daily life of the Church.

Just as, when we are at Mass, we all serve or minister to each other, so, day by day, and in all sorts of circumstances, Christians are serving their fellow human beings.

Some care for the sick; mothers and fathers care for their children and each other; teachers hand on knowledge and skills; men and women visit the poor and help them . . . You will be able to think of many more examples.

To the Mass we bring our acts of service, the failures as well as the successes. We offer them to the Father, through his Son Jesus. The Mass is a celebration of our everyday lives.

From the Mass we take the power to serve the world.

Serving is praying

Praying is talking to God. At least, that is one way of praying. Praying is also listening to God.

Praying is not only done with words. It can be done in complete silence and peace — happy just to be with God.

Praying can be done with the whole body. For example, to make the sign of the cross, to genuflect, are ways of praying with the body. We often call that way of praying 'worship'.

When people get together to worship we call it 'liturgy'. Liturgy is the community praying, worshipping together in words and actions.

So, when we serve at the altar, we are praying. When we lead the priest from the sacristy to the sanctuary, or stand holding a candle while the Gospel is read, we are praying.

Praying together

By our altar serving, we are doing our bit to build up the worship of the whole community.

The liturgy of the Mass is like putting up a building. The priest lays the foundation stone. By the power he has received at his ordination, he makes the sacrifice of the Mass present and effective.

A foundation stone is there to be built upon. We, all of us, are the bricklayers. The bricks are our worship. Each of us contributes to the building up of the worship of the whole community.

As an altar server, we play an important part in that building up. We have our own 'bricks' of worship to place along with everybody else's.

A building with faulty bricks, or badly-laid bricks, can be ugly and dangerous.

When we are serving at the altar, therefore, we give of our best. We serve with care, dignity and prayer.

That way we will be serving not only the priest, but the entire Church, helping it to give praise and honour to God.

Chapter 2

What is the Mass about?

We go to Mass on Sundays
- because we are God's family
- to hear what he has to say to us
- to speak to him in prayer

How did it all start? What does it mean?

Before the time of Jesus

Once every year, for thousands of years, Jewish families have eaten a special meal. It is called the Passover meal. That was the meal Jesus ate with his apostles the night before he died — the meal we call the Last Supper.

The Jews celebrate the Passover meal to remind themselves how God loved them and rescued them from being slaves in Egypt. He rescued them, promised to be with them for ever, and led them to the Promised Land, Israel.

The Last Supper

When Jesus sat down with his apostles for the Passover meal he spoke of all the wonderful things God had done for his people. He told his friends, the apostles, that God was about to do even greater things for them.

First, he washed the feet of the apostles, as we saw in Chapter 1. It was as though he was saying, 'Whatever wonderful gifts are given to you, always take care to serve one another'. Then Jesus told his apostles that soon he would leave them. They were not to be sad, Jesus said, because the Holy Spirit would come to them to help them carry on his work.

During the meal, Jesus gave his friends a wonderful gift — he gave himself, his own body and blood. Taking some bread, he said a prayer to his Father, broke it and gave a piece to each apostle. He said, 'This is my body'.

Later in the meal he picked up his cup of wine, again prayed to his Father and gave each apostle the cup to drink from. He said, 'This is my blood'.

What the Last Supper meant

The old Passover meal told of the rescuing of God's people from slavery in Egypt. The Last Supper — the *new* Passover meal — tells of the rescuing of God's people from slavery to sin.

The body and blood which Jesus gave to his apostles was the same body and blood he offered to his Father when he died on the cross. By that sacrifice our sins are forgiven, and we are given a share in the life of Jesus.

The Last Supper and the Mass

When Jesus gave the bread and wine — his body and blood — to the apostles, he gave them a command.

'Do this in memory of me'.

We obey that command every time we celebrate the Mass.

At Mass, we offer to the Father the sacrifice of Jesus. He makes us part of that sacrifice, and we receive the same benefits as if we had been at the Last Supper, or at the Cross, with Jesus.

Of course, the Mass today looks very different from the Last Supper, nearly two thousand years ago. The style is different, but the meaning is the same.

The Mass today

The Mass has many different parts and different moods. We can be better and more useful altar servers if we know

'Do this in memory of me'

something of what those parts mean. Let's take a look at them.

The Mass has five main parts. Here is an easy way to remember them:

- Come
- Listen
- Give thanks
- Take and eat
- Go

Try to imagine that it is God — Father, Son and Spirit — who speaks these commands.

Come

God invites us to come together at Mass. Boys and girls, men and women, lay people and priests — we come to the altar of God. From our homes, our jobs, our play, God calls us together as one family.

This part of the Mass — *Come* — works this way:

Song at the Entry: Singing together unites us more closely. It also sets a mood for the whole Mass.

Greeting: The priest makes the Sign of the Cross. Then he greets everybody and we all reply together, showing that the Lord is with us and makes us one.

Penitential Rite: We tell God and each other we are sorry for our sins. The things we do wrong divide us. If we are sorry, God forgives us and so we become more of a family.

'Glory to God in the highest . . .': Together we praise God for all the wonderful things he has done for us.

Opening Prayer, or Collect: Now that we have answered God's invitation to 'Come' and we have come together as one people, we pray together. The priest says the words on our behalf, and we answer Amen.

Listen

The Mass is a kind of conversation between God and ourselves. He speaks to us and we reply in our prayers and songs. This goes on during the whole of the Mass, but the most obvious time that God speaks to us is in what we call the Liturgy of the Word.

Here are the main parts of *Listen:*

Readings: Two or three passages from the Bible are read out. The final one is always from a Gospel — the words and life of Jesus. The Bible is the Word of God. It is the voice of God, telling us about himself and teaching us how to live.

Responsorial Psalm: This is an ancient song-prayer from the Bible. It is chosen so that we can pray about the first reading, which we have just heard.

Gospel Acclamation: Just before the reading of the Gospel, we sing a short verse which is really a shout of joy. Some-

times it is sung a second time, after the Gospel. It begins with the word Alleluia, except during Lent.

Homily: The priest or deacon explains some part of the readings. This is to help us put God's teaching into practice in our own lives.

Creed: Beginning with the words 'We believe in one God', we together tell out loud what we believe about God and the Church.

Bidding Prayers, or Prayer of the Faithful: Usually the priest starts and finishes these, and a reader announces about five things for us to pray about. The five mini-prayers often take their theme from something in the readings or the homily and link it with our daily lives. After each one, we pray in silence, and then out loud together, with words like 'Lord graciously hear us'.

These first two sections of the Mass, *Come* and *Listen,* take place mainly while the priest is at his chair and the reader is at the lectern. At the end of the Bidding Prayers, the priest goes to the altar.

Give Thanks

When we look around at the wonderful world God has made — when we think of all the good things God has done for each one of us — most of all, when we remember the teaching and work of Jesus, *then* we must thank God for his great goodness to us.

Thanking God is the most important part of this section of the Mass, which all happens at or near the altar.

Here are the parts of *Give Thanks:*

Preparation of the Gifts, or Offertory: This is exactly like getting the table ready for a meal. Things such as the chalice and Missal are placed on the altar.

Most important of all, bread and wine are brought in procession to the altar by a few people, who represent us all. Bringing up the bread and wine is a sign that we want to thank God by offering him all that we have, all that we are. The wonderful thing is that God changes the bread and wine into the body and blood of his Son, Jesus.

So, when the priest raises up these offerings he says that the bread 'will become for us the bread of life', and the wine 'will become our spiritual drink'.

Eucharistic Prayer means Thanksgiving Prayer. It is the most important prayer of the entire Mass. We thank the Father for everything he has ever done for us. We especially thank him for Jesus.

It starts with the priest saying to us 'The Lord be with you' and 'Let us give thanks to the Lord our God'.

During the Eucharistic Prayer, we remember the dying, the rising and ascending to heaven of Jesus. We pray for the whole Church, those who are alive and those who are dead.

During the Eucharistic Prayer, the bread and wine become the body and blood of Jesus.

The Prayer ends when the priest says to the Father for us all,

> Through him (that is, through Jesus), with him, in him, in the unity of the Holy Spirit,
> all glory and honour is yours, almighty Father,
> for ever and ever.

We answer

> Amen.

'Through, with and in Jesus': this is the most complete prayer. It gets its power from him; he is present in it.

Take and eat

At the Last Supper, Jesus said the bread was now his body, and the wine was now his blood. He added, 'Take and eat', 'Take and drink.' So, at Mass, we obey that command of Jesus. At Communion, we eat and drink the body and blood of Jesus Christ.

Here are the parts of *Take and Eat:*

The *'Our Father'* is the ideal prayer to begin this part of the Mass. It is our Father in heaven who feeds us with our daily bread and at the same time forgives us our sins.

The *Sign of Peace* reminds us that before we receive Jesus in communion we must be at peace with everybody. We turn to the people nearest to us and shake their hands as a sign of the peace and love that Jesus wants us to share.

Communion is a simple action. What could be more simple than eating and drinking? But it means much more than an ordinary meal. Through communion we receive the life of Jesus Christ and we are united with all the other people who receive him. Communion makes us one.

Being one with Jesus in this way is so important that we spend a few moments praying to him in the silence of our hearts.

Go

'Go in peace, to love and serve the Lord.' After a final song, we really do go. But that is not the end of it all.

In Chapter 1 we said the Mass is a reflection of how we ought to live. Now that the Mass is over, we must go and live in a new way: Jesus' way.

We should:
- be sorry for what we do wrong and be quick to forgive others *(Penitential Rite)*
- be ready to listen to what God has to say to us *(Liturgy of the Word)*
- be regular in praying *(Eucharistic Prayer)*
- be ready to share with friends and strangers *(Communion)*.

This what the Mass is all about.

Chapter 3
Hints on Serving

People who serve

First, here are some of the jobs altar servers are asked to do.

Acolyte: This is the server who does most to help the priest. Acolytes usually serve in pairs, and at solemn Mass they carry candles at the beginning and end of the Mass, as well as at the gospel.

Cross-bearer: The server who carries the processional cross at the beginning and end of the service and at other processions.

Thurifer: Server who carries the thurible. Sometimes accompanied by a boat bearer, who carries an incense boat.

MC: Master of Ceremonies — the server who guides and helps other servers to do their job well.

Before serving

Check the serving list, or rota, every week to make sure you know when you are due to serve. If you cannot attend for any reason, tell the MC, or arrange a substitute in good time.

Before leaving home, make sure you are neat and tidy. Wear black shoes, if you can. If you do not have black shoes, some other dark colour is preferable. Trainers, or tennis shoes, should not normally be worn for serving. Try to avoid brightly coloured socks.

Arrive at the church in good time, 15 minutes before Mass is due to begin.

In the sacristy everyone should be as quiet as possible. Check that your cassock and cotta, or alb, fit you and that they are clean and neat.

While serving

Hands are held joined together, in front of your chest, when you are standing, walking, or kneeling and you have nothing to carry.

The best way of doing this is to hold your hands palm against palm and at right angles to each other — but with the fingers curled around the other hand.

When one hand is being used to hold something (for example, the water-cruet) the other hand should be laid flat on your chest. Never let your spare hand hang down at your side.

Eyes should always be on the priest, or the reader when he or she is reading, and the senior server. Never stare at the people in the church, or gaze around. You have an important job to do and so you need to be on the watch for what you must do next.

Walking in procession or across the sanctuary is always to be calm and dignified. Neither a rush nor a crawl.

If you are walking with other servers or the priest, keep together and act as a team.

You may sometimes set off walking then realise you have made a mistake. Maybe you should not have moved, or you have gone to the wrong place. Don't worry. Calmly go back to your place as if nothing had gone wrong. Few people will notice, if you don't rush.

Genuflecting is done by kneeling on your right knee for a second. Your right knee should touch the floor alongside your left heel.

Keep your hands together and your back straight and genuflect fairly slowly. It should not be a quick 'bob'.

New servers often need to practise genuflecting until they get the hang of it.

When do you genuflect? It all depends where the tabernacle is located in your church. If it is in the sanctuary, you genuflect when you arrive at the start of the service and when you leave at the end. If the tabernacle is placed elsewhere in the church and you pass it on your way to and from the sanctuary you should genuflect when you pass it. The priest or senior server will make sure everybody does the same thing.

Bowing is a moderate bending of the head and shoulders. Neither a nod nor a doubling up.

You bow to the altar when you enter and leave the sanctuary, if there is no tabernacle there. You sometimes bow when you turn away from the priest; for example, after you have helped him wash his fingers. It is not necessary to bow every time you pass the priest.

Sitting: When you sit, keep your back straight and your hands on your knees. Crossed legs and fidgetting are signs of a poor server.

Kneel: Always with your back quite straight. Do not sit on your heels.

When changing from kneeling to sitting, or sitting to kneeling, always stand up first. Do not slide off the front of your seat. Do not use your hands to push yourself up, or support yourself as you change position.

Turning: When two servers are together they should usually turn inwards towards each other.

Particular hints

Acolytes work in twos. When carrying candles, the outside hand holds the candlestick under its knob and the inside hand is placed under the base. When you accompany the processional cross, do not bow or genuflect.

Cross-bearer: Because the cross is so important you do not bow or genuflect when carrying it. Make sure the figure on the cross faces to the front. Hold it high enough so that you do not catch the base with your ankles, it can be painful.

Thurifer: Before incense is put in — hold the thurible with your left hand, under the plate at the top of the chains. The right hand is then free to slide open the cover of the thurible and then to lift the lower part so that the priest may easily put in the incense. When you are swinging the thurible it is best to hold it with your right hand.

Book-bearer: Often a server is required to hold a book while the priest reads from it. You do so by placing your hands under the bottom edges of the opened book (with its open pages facing away from you!) and your thumbs supporting the back of the book so that it is upright.

Allow the priest to raise or lower the book so that he can read more easily.

Torchbearers: Torches are always held in the outside hand (with the other hand on your chest). While in procession, the bottom of the candlestick should be just clear of the floor. When you are kneeling or standing, the bottom of the candlestick rests on the floor.

Serving means teamwork — working with the priest and other servers. Be alive to what the priest is doing. Be aware of your fellow servers.

• Move quietly
• Act calmly
• Do not call attention to yourself

Which means: serve reverently.

Chapter 4
How to serve at Mass

The Catholic Church has many rules about how to serve at Mass. Most of them are contained in the Introduction to the Roman Missal (known as The General Instruction).

Because church buildings differ so much from each other and because different places have different customs it is not possible to lay down exact rules for the way everybody should serve, in every church and situation. The parish priest is the final authority on serving at Mass in your parish.

What you will find set out here are the basic rules with a few suggestions.

Simple form of serving Mass

(These instructions assume you are serving by yourself. Sometimes the various actions will be shared between two or more servers.)

Getting ready

When you arrive at the church, pause for a moment or two to say a prayer. Then go to the sacristy and put on your cassock and cotta, or alb.

Check the sanctuary. The following things need to be there before Mass begins:

Missal
*Lectionary
 bidding prayers

bowl, water, and towel for the priest's fingers
corporal
purificator(s)
chalice(s)
*bread
*wine

candles
cross
(missal stand or cushion)
(bell)

tabernacle key

Items in brackets are optional.

Items marked * are sometimes carried to the sanctuary during the Mass:

- *Lectionary* may be carried in procession from the sacristy by a reader or a deacon. Sometimes the deacon carries a Book of the Gospels.
- *Bread and wine* may be carried up at the Offertory procession. Make sure they are in their proper place before Mass begins.

In the sacristy, be ready to help the priest in any way he may ask. When ready, recite the prayer before serving Mass.

Mass begins: Come

The server leads the priest (and the reader and/or deacon, if there is one) to the sanctuary.

Stop at the foot of the steps to the altar.

Step to one side so that the priest can stand in the centre.

All bow or genuflect together.

Where there is limited space the servers may have to precede the priest into the sanctuary and genuflect before him.

Allow the priest to move away first, if this is the custom in your parish, then go to your 'base'. The 'base' is the place where a server spends most of the time during Mass.

Take the open Missal to the priest, if he requires it. Otherwise stand, and listen and respond to the prayers.

When you take the Missal to the priest, go straight to him; pause when you get just in front of him and hold the book up so that he can read from it easily.

Liturgy of the Word: Listen
Sit to listen to the readings.

Stand for the Gospel Acclamation. (It often starts with the word Alleluia.)

Stand facing the place where the Gospel is being read.

When the priest or deacon says, 'A reading from . . . etc' make a sign of the cross with your thumb on your forehead, lips and chest.

Sit for the homily.

Stand for the Creed, if it is said.

Carry the book of Bidding Prayers to the priest, if he needs it, and return with it at the end.

Liturgy of the Eucharist: Give thanks
Preparation of the Gifts: the Offertory
Servers may place on the altar:
- corporal
- Missal (on its stand or cushion, if needed)
- chalice(s)
- purificator(s)

The corporal is opened fully in the centre of the altar, with its edge lying along the edge of the altar where the priest is to stand.

The Missal is placed to the left of the open corporal.

Chalices and purificators are placed on the altar to the right of the corporal.

The priest may wish to spread the corporal himself. If so, carry the corporal and chalice together to the altar; hand them to the priest, or place them on the altar where he can easily take them.

If there is no Offertory procession, pick up the cruets from the credence-table, water in the left hand, wine in the right hand. Stand at the end of the altar in such a way that the priest can easily take the cruets from you.
Wine is handed first and received back.
Then the water.
Turn and return to the credence-table.
Put the cruets down.

If there is an Offertory procession, go with the priest, stand on his right, and help him if he hands on to you any of the gifts. Do not take them directly from the people who are in the procession.

Place the gifts on the altar where the priest can easily reach them.

If the collection money is brought up, do not place it on the altar but in some other place, such as the credence-table.

Fetch the water cruet and hand it to the priest when he needs it. When he has finished with it, take it and the wine cruet to the credence-table and put them down.

At all Masses, place the towel, unfolded, on your left arm, pick up the bowl with your left hand and the water jug or cruet in your right hand.

Return to the altar and stand so that the priest does not have to reach you over the top of the altar. Raise the bowl so that the priest does not have to bend down. Pour water on his fingers and hands until he gives a signal to stop. Allow him to take the towel off your arm and make it easy for him to put it back there again.

Turn and return to the credence-table; place cruet, bowl and towel there.

Return to your 'base'.

Eucharistic Prayer
Kneel at the end of the 'Holy, holy, holy' until after the Great Amen (just before the 'Our Father').

However in some places the custom is to kneel only for the consecration.

Also in some churches the bell is rung by the server when the priest raises the Bread and Wine at the consecration.

Rite of Communion: Take and eat
Sign of Peace: be prepared to go to the priest and make the Sign of Peace (handshake).

When the *Lamb of God* is finished, all kneel.

When the priest has finished saying 'Behold the Lamb of God', pause until he has given himself communion from the chalice, then stand and go forward to receive communion. The best place for this is where you stand to help the priest wash his fingers. Return to your 'base' and wait until communion is almost finished.

When the priest has only two or three more communions to give, stand and go to the credence-table, pick up the water cruet and when the priest has returned to the centre of the altar (he may have to go to the tabernacle first), carefully pour water into the chalice until he tells you to stop. Turn away and take the water cruet back to the credence-table.

Return to the altar and take the chalice, corporal, purificator and any ciboria to the credence-table.

In some churches the priest washes the chalice and ciboria (this action we call 'purification') at the credence-table; be ready to help there. Sometimes all this is left until after the Mass is ended.

Concluding Rites: Go

When the priest has given the final blessing and announced the *dismissal* ('The Mass is ended . . .') walk around to the front of the altar and stand at the foot of the steps leading to it.

Wait for the priest. Genuflect or bow together, turn and lead the priest back to the sacristy by the way you came at the beginning of Mass.

In the sacristy: often, the priest and servers bow to the Cross and then to each other. Wait until the priest gives you a signal to go. Bring back to the sacristy the chalice, any ciboria, the cruets, bowl and cloths.

Put out the candles, tidy the sanctuary and cover the altar with its dust cloth, if there is one at your church.

Take off your cassock and cotta, or alb, hang them neatly in their place. Say a brief prayer as you pass through the church.

Solemn form of serving Mass

Getting ready

When you arrive at the church pause for a moment or two to say a prayer. Then go to the sacristy and put on your cassock and cotta, or alb.

Check the sanctuary. The following things need to be there before Mass begins:

Missal
*Lectionary
bidding prayers

bowl, water, and towel for the priest's fingers
corporal
purificator(s)
chalice(s)
*bread
*wine

*candles
*cross
(missal stand or cushion)
(bell)

tabernacle key

Items in brackets are optional.

Items marked * are often carried to the sanctuary during the Mass:

- *Lectionary* may be carried in procession from the sacristy by a reader or deacon. Sometimes the deacon carries a Book of Gospels.

- *Bread and wine* may be carried up at the Offertory procession. Make sure they are in their proper place before Mass begins.

- *Cross and candles* may be carried by servers as part of the entry procession.

In the sacristy, be ready to help the priest in any way he may ask. When everybody is ready all recite together the prayer before serving Mass. Remember that you will be serving as part of a team.

Mass begins: Come

At a more solemn Mass:

> The priest puts incense in the thurible before leaving the sacristy.
>
> The order of procession is as follows

	thurifer	
acolyte 1	cross	acolyte 2
	other servers	

reader or deacon carrying lectionary or Book of the Gospels

priest

Arriving at the sanctuary all bow or genuflect in twos, except the cross-bearer and the acolytes (see previous chapter).

Thurifer stands to one side and waits for the priest.

Cross-bearer and acolytes place the cross and candles in the places assigned:

- the cross may be placed in a stand near the altar or at the side of the sanctuary;

- the candles may be placed on the altar (if they are small enough)

  or on the floor near the altar

  or on the credence-table.

Cross-bearer and acolytes go to their sanctuary 'base'. The acolytes are normally based close to the credence-table. The 'base' is the place where a server spends most of the time during Mass. Other servers go to their 'base', usually at the side of the sanctuary.

Reader or deacon places the Book on the altar.

Priest, after his bow or genuflection, kisses the altar. He then usually goes to the other side of the altar.

Thurifer comes to the priest, hands the boat to the deacon or MC, opens the thurible and lifts it up so that the priest may put incense into it. The thurifer closes the thurible and hands it to the priest.

Priest censes the altar by walking around it, pausing on the way to cense the cross. Or he censes the cross just before walking around the altar.

Priest gives the thurible back to thurifer and goes to his chair. Thurifer takes thurible away and hangs it up (in the sacristy or some other place). It will not be needed again until just before the Gospel. Thurifer returns to his 'base'.

Priest begins the Mass and all the servers make the sign of the cross with him and respond to the greetings and prayers. The Missal should be open and ready so that a server may take it to the priest as soon as he requires it.

Liturgy of the Word: Listen

All servers sit and listen to the Readings.

At the end of the Reading before the Gospel, the thurifer fetches the thurible. This may be done before the Reading, but no server should move while a Reading is taking place.

Acolytes pick up their candles.

Thurifer leads acolytes and stands in front of the priest. *or* Acolytes and thurifer go separately to the priest, if this is necessary. Try to keep unnecessary movement down to a minimum.

Thurifer hands the incense boat to the deacon or MC, opens the thurible and holds it while the priest puts incense in. Thurifer then closes thurible and stands back or to one side, ready to lead the procession to the lectern.

Deacon or priest joins the acolytes.

At a signal, all proceed to the lectern.

Procession to lectern

	Thurifer	
Acolyte 1	Priest/Deacon	Acolyte 2

At the lectern the acolytes stand alongside the Book, facing each other, or in another convenient place dictated by the lay-out of the sanctuary.

Thurifer stands to one side of the deacon or priest, ready to hand over the thurible after he has said 'A reading from the holy Gospel according to . . . .'

At the end of the Gospel the thurifer leads the acolytes and the deacon or priest back the way they have come.

Thurifer returns the thurible to its 'base'.

Acolytes also return their candles to their normal place (credence-table or altar).

All servers return to their 'base'. All servers sit and listen to the homily.

All stand for the Creed.

A server may be required to hold the book of bidding prayers for the priest.

Liturgy of the Eucharist: Give thanks

Preparation of the Gifts: Offertory

Servers may place on the altar:
• corporal (unfolded)
• Missal and its stand
• chalice(s)
• purificator(s)

The corporal is opened fully in the centre of the altar, with its edge lying along the edge of the altar where the priest is to stand.

The Missal is placed to the left of the open corporal.

Chalices and purificators are placed on the altar to the right of the corporal.

Servers should not normally lead the procession to the priest. The Procession of the Gifts is an action solely for the members of the congregation.

When the people bring the offerings to the priest, acolytes or other servers may help the priest if his hands are full. Bread and wine are placed on the altar but not the money from the collection.

Servers assist the priest by handing him cruets of water and wine.

Thurifer goes out to prepare the thurible during the first part of the Preparation of the Gifts and returns with it straight away.

At the altar, after the priest has raised the chalice and said 'Blessed are you, Lord God . . .', the thurifer opens the thurible for incense to be put in. This is done in the same way as at the beginning of the Mass.

When the priest has finished censing the gifts, the altar and the crucifix, he himself is censed by the deacon, or, if there is no deacon, a senior server, or the thurifer. After the priest has been censed, the acolytes present the finger bowl, water, and towel for him to wash his fingers.

Thurifer may cense other priests, servers and congregation.

Thurifer then stands to the side of the sanctuary, if incense is to be used at the elevation of the consecrated Bread and Wine. Otherwise the thurifer takes the thurible away. It will not be needed again.

Eucharistic Prayer
All servers kneel after the 'Holy, holy, holy,' until the Great Amen (that is, immediately before the 'Our Father'). However in some places the custom is to kneel only for the consecration.

The bell is rung in some places when the priest elevates (lifts up high) the consecrated bread and the chalice.

If incense is used during the Eucharistic Prayer, a senior server puts incense in the thurible. This should be done during the 'Holy, holy, holy' so that everybody may concentrate upon the words and actions of the priest without distraction during the Eucharistic Prayer.

Thurifer kneels to one side of the altar — not in the centre where the people might be distracted. The consecrated Bread and Wine are censed by the thurifer with three swings of the thurible when the priest raises them at the elevation. Thurifer should remain in the sanctuary until the end of the Eucharistic Prayer.

Rite of Communion: Take and eat

The *Sign of Peace* is exchanged by servers with their nearest companions only.

Communion is received prayerfully and quietly at the place indicated by the priest or the senior server. After receiving communion servers should spend a few moments in quiet prayer while communion is given to the rest of the community.

As communion comes to an end, two servers prepare to help the priest or deacon clean the chalice and ciboria by handing the cruet of water and taking away the dried things and placing them on the credence-table. All this can take place at the credence-table, or at the end of the altar. Sometimes the chalice, ciboria and patens are placed on the credence-table and left there for purification after Mass has ended.

Concluding Rites: Go

The priest says the postcommunion prayer. For this he will need the Missal. If he is standing at his chair, a server takes the Missal to the priest as at the opening prayer. Otherwise it will be placed on the altar.

The procession back to the sacristy is like the entry procession except that the thurifer walks with the other servers behind the cross and acolytes.

In preparing for the exit, servers should take care not to move while the priest is reciting the final prayer or the blessing.

There are several ways of departing from the sanctuary:

1 Cross and acolytes go together to the centre of the sanctuary, face the altar, pause, turn and slowly begin the procession. Don't go too fast; gaps will appear in the line. Other servers come in pairs to the centre, face the altar, bow or genuflect, turn and follow the cross and acolytes.

2 All servers stand in a line across the sanctuary (if there is room) with the cross and acolytes in the centre and bow or genuflect with the priest.

3 Cross and acolytes lead the other servers and ministers
   down the centre aisle and when all are out of the sanctuary they turn to the altar, bow or genuflect, turn and
   proceed to the sacristy.

Of the three methods, number 1 is preferable. Number 2
can be very untidy. Number 3 often results in many
servers being half-way back to the sacristy before they bow
or genuflect.

In the sacristy: often the priest and servers bow to the
Cross and then to each other. All wait quietly until the
priest or a senior server gives the signal to disperse. Clear
and tidy the sanctuary, take off cassock and cotta, or alb
and depart.

Pause for a short prayer on your way out of the church.

Chapter 5
The Meaning of Things in Church

This is a list of some of the things we see or use in church with a brief explanation of their meaning.

Acolytes' candlesticks: Carried by acolytes, these have a base so that they can stand on their own.

Aisle: *See* NAVE.

Alb: A white, full-length gown with sleeves and sometimes a hood. It is always worn by a priest at Mass, and by servers in some churches.

Altar: The stone or wooden table where the most important part of the Mass, the Eucharistic Prayer, takes place. Very often the altar contains relics (remains of saints) which were placed there when the altar was dedicated.

At Mass it is covered with a long white cloth and sometimes candles are placed there, though these may stand on the floor. A crucifix may be on the altar, or there may be one hanging from the ceiling, or a processional cross may be used instead. The altar is one of the three most important places in the celebration of Mass. The others are the CHAIR and the LECTERN.

Altar Bread: *See* HOST.

Ambo: The reading desk where the reader, deacon and priest proclaim the readings from the Bible. It is very often called a LECTERN. A PULPIT is for the same purpose but it is much larger and is usually somewhere outside the sanctuary.

Amice: An oblong, white cloth with two tapes which the priest sometimes wears around his shoulders, underneath the alb.

Boat: Container for INCENSE.

Burse: A coloured and decorated 'envelope' which contains the CORPORAL. Not often used today.

Candlestick: The holder for lighted candles. Some are designed to be carried by servers.

Cassock: Full-length gown with sleeves worn by servers and priests. The most common colour is black but it can sometimes be red. Bishops' cassocks are purple, cardinals' are scarlet and the Pope's is white.

Chair: The priest has a special chair to signify that he is the leader of the congregation. It should be placed behind, or to one side of the altar. It is one of the three most important places in the celebration of Mass. The others are the LECTERN and the ALTAR.

Chalice: The cup which contains the Precious Blood. Most chalices are made of precious metal.

Chalice Veil: A coloured and decorated cloth which covers the chalice when it stands on the credence-table.

Chasuble: The outer garment worn by the priest at Mass. There are different colours for the different seasons and feasts:

white	violet
red	black
green	rose

- *White* is used on:
  feasts of Our Lord (except the Passion)
  feasts of Our Lady, angels and saints who were not martyrs
  All Saints (November 1st)
  John the Baptist (June 24th)
  John the Evangelist (December 27th)
  The Chair of St Peter (February 22nd)
  Conversion of St Paul (January 25th)
  Masses for the Dead (sometimes)

- *Red* is used on:
  Palm Sunday
  Good Friday and Feasts of the Passion of Our Lord
  Pentecost and Masses of the Holy Spirit
  Feasts of apostles, evangelists and martyrs

- *Green* is used:
  In Ordinary Time

- *Violet* is used in:
  Lent
  Advent
  Masses for the dead (sometimes)

- *Black* is used in:
  Masses for the Dead (sometimes)

- *Rose* is used on:
  Third Sunday of Advent (Gaudete Sunday)
  Fourth Sunday of Lent (Laetare Sunday)

  See also YEAR, liturgical.

Ciborium: The container for the bread, before or after its consecration. It looks like a chalice, but has a lid.

Communion bowl: A bowl used for the distribution of communion, in place of a ciborium.

Cope: A large, full-length cape, held by a clasp at the front, worn for Benediction of the Blessed Sacrament and on other solemn occasions.

Corporal: A square, white, linen cloth on which stand the chalice, ciborium and paten from the Preparation of the Gifts until the end of Communion.

Cotta: A white, linen garment worn over the cassock. A larger and longer type of the same garment is called a SURPLICE.

Credence-table: The side table on which are placed things necessary for the Mass, such as the water cruet, towel, chalice etc.

Crucifix: A cross with the figure of Jesus on it. There is always one on or near the altar.

Cruet: A small container, usually made of glass, containing the water or wine for the Mass. Sometimes a larger jug replaces the water cruet. When communion is to be given under both kinds (that is, when all the people receive communion from the chalice as well as the host) the wine will be contained in a jug or something similar.

Dalmatic: The sleeved top garment sometimes worn by a deacon. It is in the same colour as the priest's chasuble.

Extinguisher: A small cone (usually of brass) fixed to the end of a pole and used for putting out (extinguishing) candles.

Finger-towel: The towel with which the priest dries his hands after the Preparation of the Gifts. Sometimes called a Lavabo towel.

Font: A water container, usually decorated, sometimes made of stone, where people are baptised.

Girdle: The cord which is tied around the waist by those who wear an alb. Some albs, particularly those worn by priests, no longer need a girdle.

Gospel Book: A large decorated book containing only the Gospel readings for the Mass. It is usually carried by the deacon.

Holy Water bucket: A container for carrying Holy Water. A sprinkler is provided so that the priest or deacon may sprinkle people and objects with the water.

Host: Strictly speaking, the consecrated bread. In practice, the name is often used for the unconsecrated altar bread. The priest's host is often larger than the others.

Humeral Veil: A long, rectangular garment, held by a clasp at the front, worn by the priest or deacon when carrying a CIBORIUM or MONSTRANCE containing the Blessed Sacrament.

Incense: A substance, looking like coarse sand, which when sprinkled on burning charcoal, gives off clouds of sweet-smelling smoke. It is contained in a BOAT; so called because of its shape.

Lavabo bowl: The bowl used when the priest washes his fingers.

Lavabo towel: Finger-towel used when the priest washes his fingers.

Lectern: The reading desk at which the reader, priest and deacon proclaim the readings from the Bible. It is sometimes called an AMBO. A PULPIT may also be used for this purpose. The Lectern is one of the three most important places in the celebration of Mass. The others are the ALTAR and the CHAIR.

Lectionary: Large book in which are contained the Readings from the Bible for the Liturgy of the Word.

Missal: The book from which the prayers of the Mass are read by the priest. Its correct name is Roman Missal. It is also sometimes called 'Sacramentary'.

Monstrance: A vessel for exposing the Blessed Sacrament. It is made of precious metal and sometimes has 'rays' coming from the centre.

Nave: The part of the church where the people sit. The passageways are called AISLES.

Pall: A square board covered in white linen to cover the chalice. It is not often used today.

Paschal Candle: A very large, decorated candle, blessed at Easter and often to be seen standing next to the baptism font. It represents the risen Christ, the light of the world.

Paten: A thin, metal plate on which is sometimes placed the bread for consecration.

Purificator: A white linen cloth which the priest uses with the chalice and ciborium. It is also used for this purpose by the deacon and other ministers of Communion.

Pyx: A container for the consecrated bread. A large pyx is kept in the TABERNACLE to hold the large host that is used for Benediction. A smaller one is used by the priest, deacon, or other ministers of Communion when taking Communion to people outside the church.

Sacramentary: A book which the priest uses at his chair and at the altar. In some countries it is the name given to the MISSAL.

Sacristy: The room where priests and servers prepare themselves for the services.

Sanctuary: The area in a church where the altar, lectern and priest's chair are placed.

Sanctuary Lamp: The lamp which is kept burning near the TABERNACLE to show that the Blessed Sacrament is present. The lamp is often in a bracket attached to the wall, or suspended from the ceiling.

Stole: A type of scarf worn by priests and deacons, which is a sign of their ministry. The priest's stole is worn around the neck. The deacon's stole is worn across the left shoulder and the ends are attached to each other on the right side.

It matches the priest's chasuble, or the deacon's dalmatic and is the same colour.

Surplice: *See* COTTA.

Tabernacle: The decorated, secure cupboard, or safe, often made of metal in which is kept the consecrated bread outside of Mass so that it may be available when sick people require Communion, or for adoration of the Blessed Sacrament. It is usually covered with a veil.

Thurible: The container for the burning charcoal and incense. It is usually suspended at the end of three chains so that it can be swung and also opened easily.

Vestments: The special clothes which are worn by priests, deacons and servers during the liturgy. For example, ALB, CHASUBLE, STOLE.

Year, Liturgical: The Church has its own calendar. The year begins on the first Sunday of Advent (four Sundays before Christmas Day).

- In the *Season of Advent,* purple vestments are worn.
- In the *Season of Christmas,* white vestments are worn. This season usually lasts for about three Sundays.
- Then *Ordinary Time* begins (this is sometimes called Sundays throughout the Year). Green vestments are worn.
- *Lent* interrupts Ordinary Time. Purple vestments are worn.
- The *Season of Easter* follows; during this time, the vestments are white.
- *Pentecost Sunday* brings the Season of Easter to an end. Red vestments are worn.
- After Pentecost, *Ordinary Time* re-starts, and the green vestments are used again. There are 33 or 34 Sundays in Ordinary Time.
- The Last Sunday in Ordinary Time is the celebration of Christ the King: white vestments are worn. This marks the end of the Church's year.
- Then the *Season of Advent* begins again.

Chapter 6
The Archconfraternity of Saint Stephen

What is the Archconfraternity?

In general terms a confraternity is a sort of club, or society, for people who are interested in the same things and want to do these things together. The Church uses the word 'confraternity' as the official name for societies set up in a parish. We often use another, easier, word instead of 'confraternity' — Guild.

An archconfraternity is a guild which has been given special power by the Church authorities in Rome. It has special privileges and facilities. Because it is an *arch*confraternity it can allow other guilds to share in those privileges and facilities.

That is what the Guild of Saint Stephen is. The main Archconfraternity is based on Westminster Cathedral, in London. It has many Guilds in parishes in Great Britain and elsewhere affiliated to it. Strictly speaking, only the Guild at Westminster Cathedral should call itself Archconfraternity, but parish Guilds call themselves branches of the Archconfraternity.

Aims and Objects

The objects of the Guild of Saint Stephen are:

- 1˙ to encourage, positively and practically, the highest standards of serving at the Church's liturgy and so contribute to the whole community's participation in a more fruitful worship of God.

- 2 to provide altar servers with a greater understanding of what they are doing so that they may serve with increasing reverence and prayerfulness and thereby be led to a deepening response to their vocation in life.

- 3 to unite servers of different parishes and dioceses for their mutual support and encouragement.

Constitution and organisation

The Archbishop of Westminster is the Superior General of the Archconfraternity and he appoints a priest to be the National Director of the Guild. He is assisted in the running of the Guild by a lay Central Council consisting of a Lay President, Vice-President, Secretary, Treasurer and other members. The Central Council is responsible for running the business side of the Guild.

Many diocesan bishops appoint a Priest Director of the Guild for their own diocese and together these form a National Council of Priest Directors, which is an advisory body to the National Director. Some dioceses have organised their own local Lay Councils to assist the Diocesan Director in furthering the work of the Guild.

The Guild may be erected in any parish with the permission of the bishop of the diocese (see Canon 312 of the new Code of Canon Law) and shall then be affiliated to the Archconfraternity at Westminster Cathedral. Thus, in each parish, while maintaining its objects and keeping the rules of the Archconfraternity, the Guild can be independent in its constitution and organisation.

Membership

Membership of the Guild is open to any server male or female, without limit of age, who can serve Mass, and who has shown a wish to live up to the objects and standards of the Guild.

It is recommended that servers should be given adequate training before being admitted to the sanctuary and then should serve satisfactorily for a minimum of six months before being enrolled as a member of the Guild. The parish priest, or the local director of the Guild, decides whether a candidate is eligible and worthy of admission to the Guild and he is empowered to perform the ceremony of enrolment and invest the server with the Guild medal, using the prescribed form of enrolment.

Rules

- 1 to serve at the altar with reverence, understanding and regularity and with due attention to personal cleanliness and tidiness.
- 2 to say short prayers in preparation for, and in thanksgiving after, serving Mass.
- 3 to observe silence in the sacristy and great reverence in the sanctuary.
- 4 to recite the Guild prayer every day.

Recommendations

We also recommend the following:

- 1 be ready to serve at every opportunity, yet making sure that your fellow servers have an equal chance.
- 2 take part in all services as fully as possible, by paying careful attention to everything that is being said or done and by joining in the prayers, responses and hymns and especially by receiving Holy Communion at Mass.
- 3 avoid doing anything which might distract the attention of the people. Do not fidget or look around, or stare at the people in the church.
- 4 carry out the ceremonies calmly and without drawing too much attention to yourself and remembering that you are part of a team.

- 5 be in good time before services so that you can prepare properly.

- 6 see that you are suitably dressed for serving (especially footwear) and that your cassock, cotta, or alb are clean and cared for.

- 7 wear the Guild Medal on all occasions when serving.

- 8 do your best to attend Guild meetings and festivals so as to get to know other servers, especially those from other parishes.

The Guild promise

I offer myself to God almighty,
to blessed Mary, our Mother
and to our holy patron, Saint Stephen.
And I promise to do my best
to serve regularly
with reverence and understanding,
for the glory of God,
the service of his Church,
and my own eternal salvation.

Becoming a Guild member

There is a special ceremony of enrolment into the Guild. As we said before, this usually happens at least six months after a server has first begun serving.

During the ceremony the server makes a solemn promise (the wording of which is given above) and is presented with the Guild Medal, which is made of bronze and is worn around the neck, hanging from a red cord.

The medal means two things:

- first, the parish priest, or local director of the Guild, has decided this particular server is eligible and worthy to be admitted to the Guild.

- second, the server accepts and wears the medal as a sign of commitment —
    commitment to serve regularly:
    commitment to serve as well as possible.

A commitment is a serious promise, and this promise is a serious one because it is made to God and the Church.

The Guild Medal

The letters XP are the first two letters of the name 'Christ' in Greek. At the top is the crown of victory given by God to everyone who overcomes evil, especially those who die for him. At the bottom are the palm branches, traditional signs of martyrs who died for Christ.

The latin words are the Guild motto: they declare that to serve at the altar is to serve Christ himself. And the reward of all good and faithful serving is a share in his kingdom.

Cui servire regnare est
To serve Christ is to reign.

Chapter 7
A Short History of the Guild

The Guild of St Stephen was founded at the beginning of this century, about the year 1901. We do not know the exact date.

Its founder was Father Hamilton MacDonald, who was chaplain at the Sacred Heart Convent at Hammersmith, in London.

Like so many of these things, the Guild started because it was needed. Father MacDonald wanted to raise the standard of altar serving, so he started regular classes for altar servers at the convent. The idea caught on, and soon he was holding meetings every month at the local parish church, Holy Trinity, Brook Green.

It was a great success. The Archbishop of Westminster, Francis Bourne (later Cardinal) was so impressed that he decided to start the Guild at Westminster Cathedral.

It was not long before Pope Pius X (later, Saint) came to hear of it. He gave the Guild his official approval in November 1905.

In 1906, the Guild of Westminster Cathedral was promoted to 'Archconfraternity'. This meant that branches of the Guild in other parishes could be linked with the one at Westminster Cathedral. In that way they could use the rules and wear the medal of the Guild. From that time on, the Guild of St Stephen began to spread very quickly.

In 1914 the great war exploded in Europe and raged until 1918. Millions of men joined the army and navy. Some of

Father Hamilton MacDonald, founder of the Guild

these were senior servers from the parishes. The result was that the Guild declined. In fact, it remained active in only one or two parishes.

But after the war, a few of Father MacDonald's 'boys' came to the rescue. They worked hard at building up the Guild again.

In 1925 Cardinal Bourne gave his approval to a new constitution for the Guild. A Central Council and an executive were established. Slowly but surely the Guild grew in numbers and in strength. Father MacDonald died in 1933; he had lived to see it firmly established.

Again, during the second great war, 1939-1945, the Guild was not able to carry on its work as in time of peace. But this time the Central Council kept things going, and when the war was over the Guild once again began to expand and grow.

Many bishops appointed a priest as diocesan director. A result of this was the formation in September 1945 of a National Council of Priest Directors to advise the National Director.

Travelling abroad was then not as common as it is today. So when in 1950 the Guild organised a pilgrimage of altar servers to Rome, it was a big adventure. And it was a great success. Since that time more Rome pilgrimages have taken place. These have varied in size from 100 to 350 servers.

Building on the wonderful work of Father Hamilton MacDonald, a number of National Directors has served the Guild with great distinction. Among these, Monsignor Edward Sutton, Monsignor Joseph Collings and Canon John Marriott will always be remembered.

In the forty years since the ending of the war of 1939-1945 the influence of the Guild has spread far and wide. There are now branches all over the British Isles. They can also be found in places as far away as Africa, Australia, Malaysia and the West Indies.

The Second Vatican Council of the Church (1963-1965) was a great challenge to the Guild of St Stephen. It meant that the Guild had to think of altar serving in a new way. Most members took up that challenge with enthusiasm and dedication. In that way they have played their part in the renewal of the Church.

The changes in the way the Mass and the rest of the liturgy are celebrated, brought about by the Second Vatican Council, have had an enormous effect on the way we serve. The style has changed. Some people even say there is no need for servers.

This is where the Guild of St Stephen can show there is still a need for good serving. It can take a lead which others will follow.

The Church works best when its members are ready and willing to serve each other. That's exactly what the Guild of St Stephen is there to do.

Chapter 8
Patrons of the Guild

St Stephen

Stephen was a brave and fearless man. He had to be, to do the work God wanted him to do.

He lived in those early days of the Church just after Jesus had returned to his Father and the Holy Spirit had come upon the Apostles at the first Pentecost.

Perhaps Stephen had actually met Jesus, heard him teaching, seen some of his miracles, even spoken to him. It is possible, but we do not know.

What we do know is that Stephen was a friend of the Apostles.

One day, an argument started up between some of the Christians in Jerusalem. Widows, who had no one to earn money for food for them, were looked after by the Church. But one group of Christians complained that the food was not being shared out fairly. So the argument started.

The Apostles were annoyed by this. 'We must get on with spreading the Good News of Jesus, not serving food', they said. 'The best way of doing God's work is by dividing up the work. So choose seven good men and they will help us in the serving'.

Everybody thought this was a good idea. They chose seven men, as the Apostles had asked, and they were officially appointed when the Apostles prayed over them and laid hands on their heads.

Top of the list of seven was Stephen. Right away he was a success. While he was doing his work of service he worked great signs and miracles. This made the enemies of the Christians very angry.

They argued with Stephen but always came off worst. They bribed some men to tell lies about Stephen and then they arrested him.

He was taken off to the Jewish council. Again, lies were told against him, and his own words were twisted out of their proper meaning.

Stephen was accused of wanting to bring an end to all the ancient customs of the Jews. He denied this. In fact, in his defence he made it obvious that the leaders of the Jews were the ones who ought to have been on trial.

Right there and then before the Council, Stephen recounted the entire history of the Jews. He said that in the past, whenever messengers had been sent by God to bring the people back from sin, those messengers had been ill-treated and sometimes they had been killed.

Worst of all, now they had killed Jesus Christ, the one all the messengers had foretold was to come to save his people.

The Jewish rulers were infuriated to hear Stephen speak like this. And when he said that he could see Jesus with God in heaven, they lost all reason and became mad with anger. They rushed at Stephen, thrust him outside the city gates, and stoned him to death.

Now Stephen showed what a great and good man he was. He had complete faith in Jesus. As the stones came crashing down on him he shouted out, 'Lord Jesus, receive my spirit'. He knew Jesus would welcome him into the Kingdom.

And as he died, Stephen did not think just of himself. He fell on his knees and prayed for those who were killing him. 'Lord, do not blame them for doing this', he prayed. Then he died.

It's a strange fact that the man who looked after the coats of those who stoned Stephen to death was a man called Saul. He thought killing Stephen was the right thing to do. But a few years later he changed his mind — or, God changed it for him. He became a Christian — one of the most famous in all history. But by then he had changed his name. He became Paul, the Apostle.

The courage and love of Stephen must have worked on Saul who became Paul.

Stephen is our patron. His courage and love can work on us too. He showed what real serving is all about. It is about working for other people, living for them. Even dying for them, in Stephen's case.

As altar servers, we serve the whole Church. Together with everybody else we use the gifts God has given us to spread the Good News. And to pray to God as one family. That is what serving is about.

A big job, but we have Stephen as our patron and our guide. We therefore pray to him to help us be good servers.

Help us, we pray you Lord,
to imitate St Stephen, your deacon,
whom we venerate as the patron of our Guild.
May we serve the Church with the same dedication
and learn to love our enemies
just as he prayed for those who persecuted him.
We ask this through Christ our Lord.

St Stephen is the principal patron of the Guild. There are others, secondary patrons. They are St Thomas More, Pope St Pius X and Our Lady.

Saint Thomas More

Thomas More was born in London in 1478. His father was a judge and Thomas followed in his footsteps. He married, had children, and was so good at his profession in the Law that he was appointed Lord Chancellor by King Henry VIII.

However, Thomas More fell out with the king and resigned. The trouble started when Henry wanted to divorce his wife. The pope refused to allow it and Thomas was loyal to the pope. Eventually he was arrested by the king, tried and beheaded at the Tower of London in 1535.

Thomas had been a very important person in the kingdom. He was always a very religious person. He served Mass every day, usually at Chelsea Old Church, on the banks of the River Thames. You can still see the church there today. Because Thomas More was such a loyal and regular Mass server, he is one of our patrons.

Pope Saint Pius X

This saintly pope is also a secondary patron of the Guild of St Stephen. He gave the Guild the Church's highest approval in 1906, so we have much to be grateful to him for.

However, that is not the main reason why he is a patron. Pius X did a great deal for the liturgy. He encouraged greater participation in the celebration of the liturgy, especially by singing. And, most of all, he made Catholics realise how important the Mass is, and how important it is to receive Holy Communion regularly at Mass. When he became pope, regular communion was not common, and children did not make their first communion until they were quite old. Pius X lowered the age at which children could make their first communion.

During the Guild's Golden Jubilee visit to Rome in 1955, Pope Pius XII recommended that Saint Pius X should be a patron of the Guild. For Pope St Pius X the Mass — and full participation in it — was the centre of everything. That is why he is one of our patrons.

Our Lady

Mary, the Mother of Jesus, is also known as the Mother of the Church. Therefore she must also be the mother of all altar servers.

All her life Mary served others. That was why she was chosen to be the Mother of God. We should pray to her to help us be better servers.

When Mary knew she was to become the mother of Jesus, she said

My soul glorifies the Lord
my spirit rejoices in God, my Saviour.
He looks on his servant in her lowliness.

Chapter 9
Some Prayers for Servers

The Guild Prayer

O God, you accept our ministry and allow us to serve at your altar; grant that while serving you we follow the example of our Patron, St Stephen, the first martyr, and that we may, like him, come to see Jesus standing at your right hand in the kingdom of heaven. We ask this through Jesus Christ, your Son.   Amen.

Alternative prayer in honour of St Stephen

Help us, we pray you Lord, to imitate St Stephen, your deacon, whom we venerate as the patron of our Guild. May we serve the Church with the same dedication and learn to love our enemies just as he prayed for those who persecuted him. We ask this through Christ our Lord.   Amen.

Prayers before serving

1 Come, O Holy Spirit, fill the hearts of the faithful and kindle in them the fire of your love.
   V. Send forth your Spirit and they shall be created.
   R. And you shall renew the face of the earth.

   O God, to whom every heart is open, every desire known and from whom no secrets are hidden; cleanse the thoughts of our hearts by the help of your Holy Spirit, that we may perfectly love you, faithfully serve you, and worthily praise your Holy Name. We ask this through Christ our Lord.   Amen.

2 O Lord, I have many interesting things that I want to do today, but please help me to remember that I am assisting at this Mass. Help me to understand that if I serve with dignity and reverence it will help the people to pray; if I serve poorly it will distract them. Help me to serve well in the name of Jesus our Lord.   Amen.

3 Father in heaven, free us from all wrong and distracting thoughts; help us to understand what we are about to do; and make us always eager to give of ourselves, that we may come worthily to your holy altar.   Amen.

Prayers after serving

1 We give you thanks Lord, for calling us to serve you. Strengthen our loyalty and keep us faithful to you, so that we may enjoy your friendship for ever.   Amen.

2 O Lord Jesus Christ, I thank you for the privilege of having served at your Altar. Now, as I leave the church, I ask that I may never forget that you are with me, wherever I may go.   Amen.

Prayers for vocations

1 Father of us all, your Spirit calls us to serve each other in the Church. Help us to discover what you want each of us to do for you, and give us the strength to do it, now and throughout our lives. We ask this through Christ our Lord.   Amen.

2 Lord Jesus Christ, grant the grace of a priestly and religious vocation to many. Inspire young people to dedicate their love, strength and work to you. Bless all those who by their generous prayers and sacrifices help God's future priests and religious.   Amen.

3 God our Father, you sent your Son, Jesus into this world and he in turn through the Holy Spirit sent the apostles to continue your work. We ask you to choose priests, brothers and sisters who will willingly give their lives in your service. We make this prayer through Christ the Lord.   Amen.